## For the designer in all of us

*Especially T.B., Connor, Vincent & Tatum*

© 2021 Center for Design Institute

Author: Linda Kuo
with Cynthia Benjamin and Paula Rees

Illustrations: Copyright © Mariana Rio
The illustrations were done in gouache and digital mixed media.

Art Direction: The Little League
(Benjamin/Kuo/Rees)

Book consultant: Charles Kim, Charlotte & Company

Book production and typography by Foreseer
Typeset in Whitney Condensed by Hoefler & Co.
Printed on Arctic Paper: Amber Graphic 150 g/m², woodfree

First Edition 2021
Library of Congress Control Number: 2021941665
ISBN 978-1-7372098-0-5

**Center for Design Books**
1325 4th Ave · Suite 1940
Seattle, Washington 98101
www.centerfordesign.net

Distributed by Six Foot Press and Ingram Publisher Services
www.sixfootpress.com | www.ingrambook.com
Printed in Turkey

***Sara Little Trouble Maker Series***

# LET TUCE GET IN TROUBLE

## LINDA KUO   MARIANA RIO

CENTER FOR DESIGN
*Books*
SEATTLE

Sara Little waving bon voyage, circa 1950.

Sara was an early Western visitor exploring places like Borneo, Malaysia, the Philippines, India, and Kenya. As a cultural anthropologist, she was always on the lookout for how people and animals solved everyday problems. She told her clients that the answers came from directly engaging with the users—to understand their needs and to observe their ways firsthand. Her design often combined these discoveries with a close look at nature's solutions, making her an early practitioner in a field now called biomimicry.

In *Lettuce Get in Trouble*, children are encouraged to explore design by developing a plan and asking good questions in order to arrive at better answers. Sara loved the foods of various cultures and introduced the U.S. to casual dining, buffets, and finger foods. She promoted small healthy snacks that were easy to make, and she knew there was little time to be spent washing the dishes.

"The excitement of my life is that I have always jumped into the unknown to find what I needed to know," Sara said. And in the process, she was not afraid to cause a little trouble with her endless curiosity driven by a need to know "why" and to make the world a better place.

Working late at her desk in 1940.

## Sara Little Turnbull
(1917-2015)

Sara Little filled way more space than she took up. She stood under five feet tall and weighed less than ninety lbs. Thus, the nickname "Little Sara," which became Sara Little—product designer, strategic planner, and teacher at Stanford's Graduate School of Business. While small in stature, she was considered a visionary giant by her clients and the many she mentored.

Raised in an impoverished household in Brooklyn, Sara was trained to look for beauty and wonder in the everyday. Her mother provided full sensory lessons on color and form by arranging fruits, vegetables, or a bouquet. When Sara was distracted by noisy neighbors, her mother would insist, "This is the music of life!" After school, she'd explore the world through the Metropolitan Museum of Art. In recognition of her unique character and creativity, Sara attended Parsons School of Design through generous community scholarships, and is featured as a notable alumna.

After college, Sara became the decor editor for *House Beautiful* magazine and leased a tiny hotel room. Her inventive ideas were published and expressed in the clever use of space, storage, color, and materials. She was influential in defining mid-century homes, products, and appliances. After her publishing career, Sara started a design consultancy that advised a long list of America's most innovative companies. Her designs ranged from medical masks to beautiful yet exceptionally functional cookware, new food stuffs, car interiors, and even space suits. She said, "I'm creating tools for living," and her objective was to save time so people could enjoy a more relaxing life.

*The men in blue suits meet with Sara Little, circa 1940.*

"When you take the time
to see, the wonders
become commonplace,
and the commonplace
become wonders."
—Sara Little

Sara watches her students becoming
teachers and smiles a giant smile.

Lin and Vince stand in the center, surrounded by their new friends and wild creations.

In a quiet corner, a little boy sees Mr. Indigo skewer pineapple wedges and cherry tomatoes onto a sugar cane.

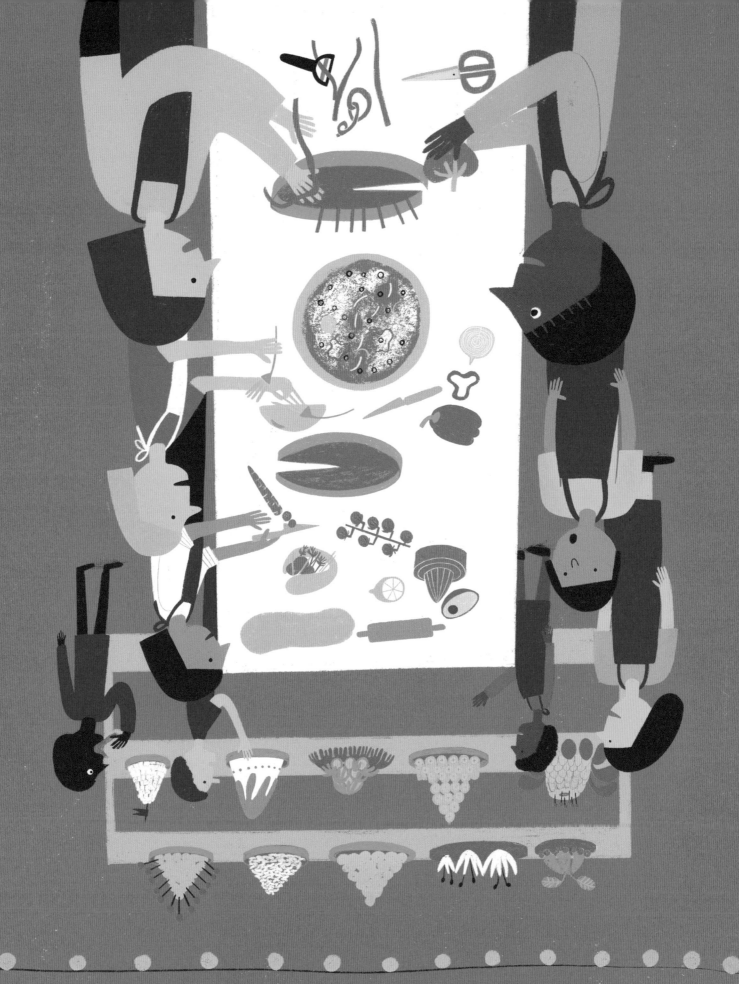

SCULPTURE & SAUCE

Vince tours some children around
the tall fennel-celeriac-kohlrabi
tower he has created.

All three look alike
but the KOHL-RA-BI
tastes like apples!

He encourages a new
friend to dunk into a
fountain of hummus
and this cheers her up.
Together, they origami
colorful dough into
a parade of pizzas
and baos.

A little boy makes sushi with white
onions and tiny purple grapes.
How many little grapes hang from
this one cluster?

One child sprinkles mint leaves
on tacos filled with bright orange
carrots and red peppers.

Lin rolls out wraps with the
children and shows off her
almond butter and
strawberry jelly burrito.

The other children get inspired,
roll up their sleeves, and start
creating new combinations.

Inside one tent are Lotus leaf plates, lettuce cups,
wild grass straws—a zero-waste lunch.

When a spring shower comes, Vince looks at the
lotus leaf and flips it over to use as an umbrella.

From continents far and near,
the children arrive in hot air balloons.

In the big park, the Little League
set up tents circling a giant
lazy Susan.

They cannot wait to
experiment and explore
the wonders inside each
tent and taste the
jewel-like vegetables.

Mr. Eggplant turns out to be the
leader of the Ministry of Food,
so he approves the party.

Why does a place setting have so many pieces?

Because eating is to celebrate life.

What you eat and how you eat tell something about you.

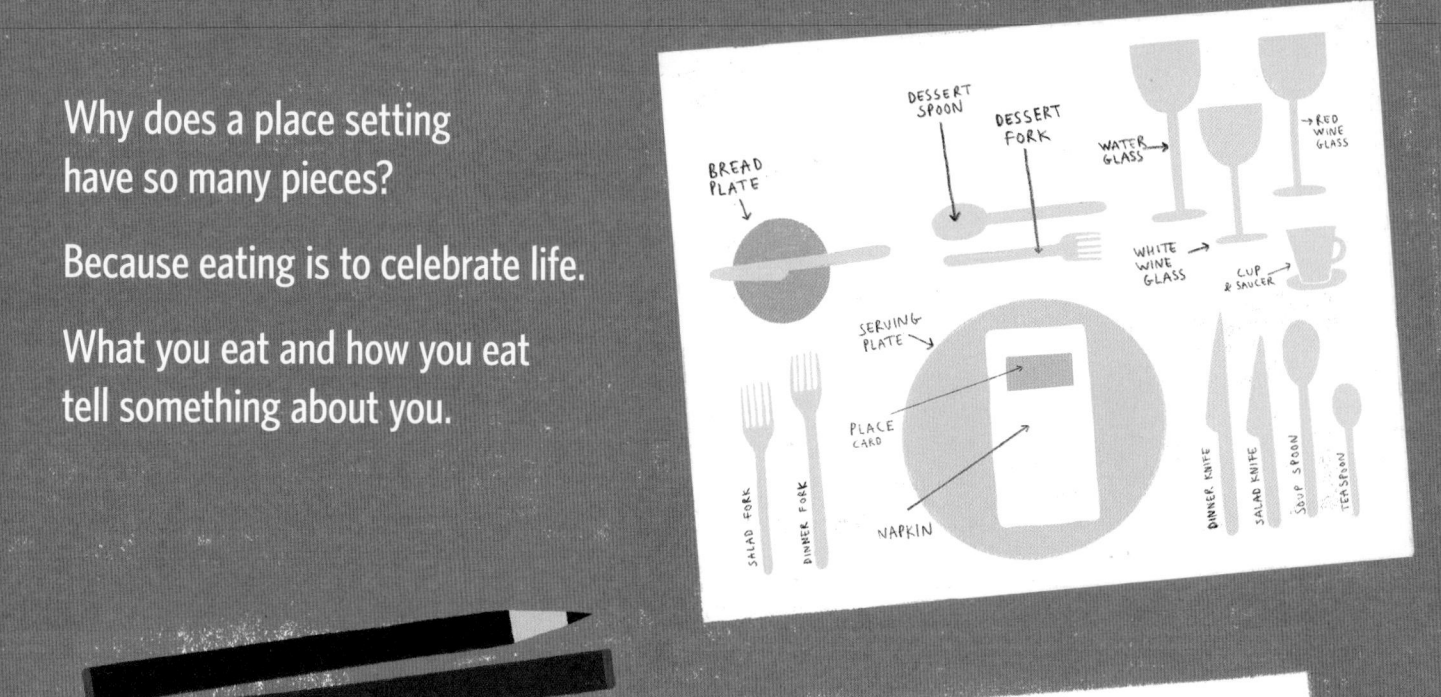

Let's build a space for people to sit around and create new foods!

Why is it important to eat vegetables?

Because vegetables are colorful,
and each color gives you a
different kind of energy.

Green for peace,
red for love,
yellow for joy.

Good design solves problems and also makes the world more beautiful and fun.

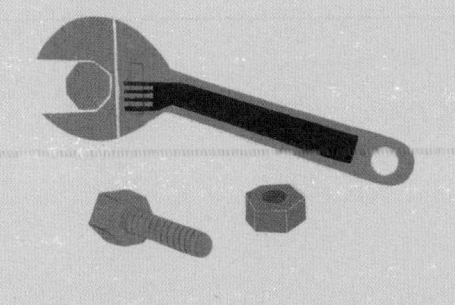

A wrench tightens nuts and bolts.

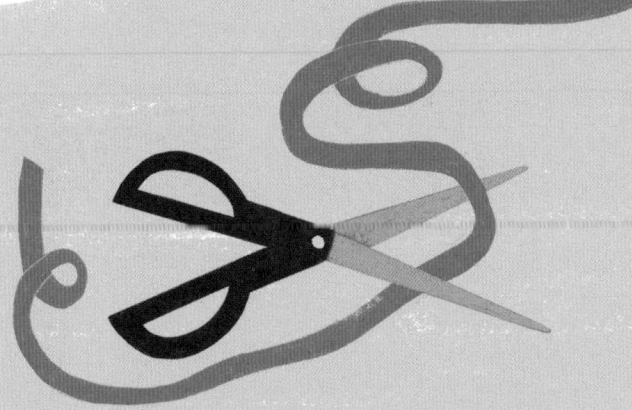

A pair of scissors cuts ribbons.

And a violin bow makes music on strings.

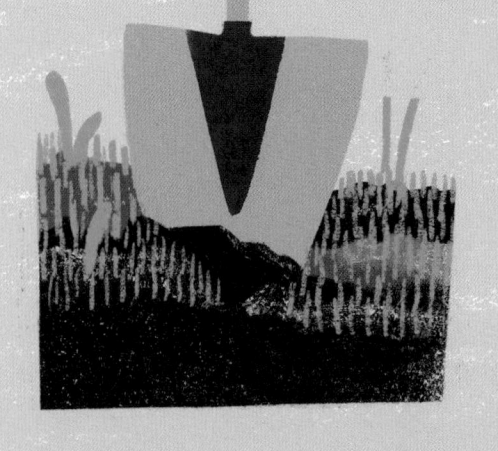

A spade turns the soil when planting a tree.

Everything around us is designed, from the clothes we wear to the spoons and plates and chairs we use.

MY friends, come to the Little Laboratory and let's design.

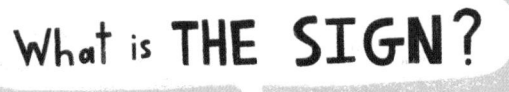

What is **THE SIGN?**

**TO DESIGN** is to look for connections!

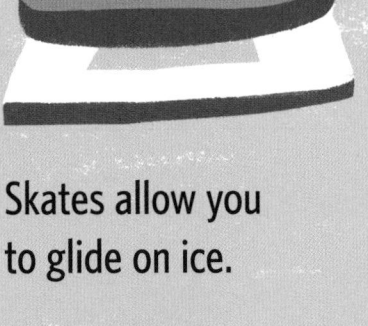

Sneakers cushion your feet for sprinting and jumping.

Skates allow you to glide on ice.

And ballet shoes help you to dance like a swan.

Boots protect your toes from rocks, twigs, and snakes when hiking in the mountains.

Sara passes by a school cafeteria. Through the windows, she sees kids with rectangular trays that hold mashed potatoes and carrots.

The broccoli is mushy. Do I have to finish this?

Can I have a grilled cheese sandwich instead?

And they must learn a sense of order!
We want you to teach these children what to eat and how to eat.
Have you talked to the children?

When Sara arrives at the gray fortress that is home to the Ministry of Food, she is welcomed by a group in dark blue suits.

The tallest gentleman, Mr. Indigo, sits her down at a long table.

One morning, a snowy white pigeon drops off a pale blue envelope with a red seal at her balcony.

MOF

Dear Sara,

Children seem to have stopped eating vegetables. We are flooded with questions from worried parents and farmers weeping over their untouched crates of cabbages, carrots, and cucumbers.

Help!
Humbly yours,
The Ministry of Food

A flurry of letters
comes to Sara daily.

A MOTHER
OF TWO TWINS

SARA LITTLE

LETTER NO. 47

Dear Sara,
I have no time to
cook and too many
plates to clean.

Help!
A Mother of Two Twins

Dear Mom of Twins,
This is serious—too many plates!
Let us start with a ONE-POT-MEAL
like chili or coq au vin, from
oven-to-table.

Sara

PS. Don't forget bananas
for dessert—they come
in natural, biodegradable
containers.

When she grows up,
asking **WHY** becomes
Sara Little's job.

When Sara was young, her wise mother would point out the shape of an egg and the curve of an eggplant.

Why does an onion have
endless layers?

Why is boiling water full
of bubbles?

Why do people eat
with forks?

Sara wears many hats
and one tiny upside-down
clock on her black turtleneck.
She is always asking a lot of questions.

Sara
is little,
young at heart,
an old soul,
with a **BIG** curiosity.